PRAISE FOR *BF...*
THEIR TF...

"These are testimoni...   ...nly in the
light of what God does, but w...   ...nd an admission
of what the Lord can do for th...   experience and interpret
God's actions."

–Robinson Onderi, Pastor, Seniorenheim Friedensau & Adventgemeinde Burg, Germany

"Reading this book will encourage and excite you to tell and live your testimony of a God that selflessly loves you, cares about you, helps you, and has an interest of saving every human being on this earth."

–Christoph Till, Pastor, Adventgemeinde Thalheim, Germany

"Undoubtedly, there is power in sharing our testimonies. No wonder Jesus encourages us to tell our stories (Mark 5:19). I believe many will be assured in their faith by reading this important book. I wholeheartedly endorse and recommend this book."

–Albert Owusu Ansah, Assistant Pastor, Emmendigen, Freiburg and Titisee-Neustadt, Germany

Because of Their Testimony

The Power of Telling Your Story

By

Chigemezi N. Wogu

FAHOLO

FAHOLO Publications

Because of their Testimony
©Copyright 2023 Chigemezi N. Wogu, *Because of Their Testimony*

Edited by Andrew Puckering

Produced and published by: BoD – Books on Demand, Norderstedt

In de Tarpen 42, 22848 Norderstedt, Germany

Bible translations used:

King James Version (KJV). Crown copyright in the UK; Public Domain overseas.

Christian Standard Bible (CSB). Copyright © 2017 by Holman Publishers. Used by permission.

Holy Bible, New International Version® Anglicised (NIV). Copyright © 1979, 1984, 2011 by Biblica, Inc.® Used by permission.

ISBN: 9783734711664

Dedicated to Chimamanda and Chiedozie. May you grow up to testify of the goodness of God and may everyone praise God because of your testimony.

CONTENTS

FOREWORD: BEING A LIVING TESTIMONY

Everybody has a story. It starts with our childhood, the way we grew up, how we chose our profession, how we met our partner, and, if we are believers, the kind of experiences we've made in our walk of faith. Usually, we tell the story of our conversion to non-believers so that they can see God's work in our lives. But sharing our testimonies not only encourages non-believers and invites them to trust in the Lord but can also be a big help for people who already are followers of Christ. It can help them to see, in the midst of their lives, how God helps, and that miracles are no illusion, but rather a reality to count on. But this requires living with God in our everyday life. It requires us to have a relationship with the Creator God, and with our Saviour, Jesus Christ.

Stories of Our Lives

Our lives involve living with God, getting answers to our prayers, experiencing miracles, and also being given the chance by Him to tell our stories. These are stories that only you have, because of the specific circumstances in which you invited the Lord into your life and started living with Him, praying to Him, going through difficult times with Him, and being changed by Him. These are stories that only you can tell in an excited and authentic way, because you lived through them and saw God working in your life, with yourself sitting in the front row, having the VIP seat.

In the following book, my good friend, colleague and former neighbour, Chigemezi Wogu, paints a picture of what testifying of Jesus does to us, to our faith, and to the people around us. It also shows how our testimonies fit in with the great cosmic conflict. Besides giving a biblical background of what being a witness means and the effects of testifying, this book also includes interesting stories from the author's own life, as well as from the lives of other people who were witnesses not only when it was comfortable, but also in the midst of trials and battles. Reading this book will encourage and excite you to tell and live your testimony of a God who selflessly loves you, cares about you, helps you, and has an interest in saving every human being on this earth. God bless you as you read, study, become excited, and share your testimonies in your home, workplace, university, school, church, or wherever you might be.

Christoph Till
Pastor, Adventgemeinde Thalheim, Germany

PROLOGUE

When I became the pastor of New Life SDA Church in Berlin, I did not know that the Lord would fill my ministry with numerous testimonies in a couple of months. Well, my testimony started even before I stepped into the position of a pastor.

I was working as a social worker with Cornelius Werk, a social work agency of the Evangelical Church in Germany. It was in a small town in the state of Sachsen Anhalt in Germany. Things were fine. I had a good salary, and I was in the process of getting a more permanent contract when the president of the Berlin Central Conference of Seventh-day Adventists in Germany called me. His request was clear: "Can you imagine becoming a pastor and working for us?" I wanted more details, and he came to our home and explained that, if I was to accept, I would need to pastor the multicultural English-speaking congregation as well as a German congregation.

I was hesitant . . . hesitant because I did not know how to tell my bosses who had been good to me that I would be leaving. Also, I had just gotten over the first difficult hurdles of becoming a social worker, whose primary job was to oversee the livelihood of kids and teenagers. My wife knew it was God's calling. Then I made a deal with God. "If you let me be released in January, I will go to work for You without asking."

When I made that prayer, I was not thinking. This was the end of October. In Germany you need to give three months' notice before you resign. The president said I could start in March the next year. I knew that starting in January was the best. So, I ended up talking to my immediate boss sometime in November, and he just said: "Well, we would like to keep you, but this is your calling; you can go at the end of December or January." He told me he would talk to the supervisor when I put things on paper.

The day I spoke with the supervisor, he was sorry to see me leave, since I had brought a different spirit of hope and thankfulness into the team. He told me I was released! I could not believe it. I shared this with the conference, and informed them I would begin in January, earlier than anticipated. They were happy; the congregation was surprised to have a new pastor by January; and God was praised.

When I told this testimony to the congregation on my first day of service, which was also the day I was installed, many were encouraged. But God had only just begun filling my ministry with testimonies. He would, through prayer, reveal how to go about leading the congregation. He would soften the minds of the church members, quell the fights and bickering that gave the congregation a bad reputation, and lead me through unknown paths. At one point, during a youth retreat, the way God surprised the young adults, and their leaders was more than amazing.

There were more testimonies to tell. In fact, I held a testimony service after I discovered that the prayer ministry, I started was bringing in answered prayers. It was the same time I told God to give me more testimonies. If He did, I would write a book about them. I must have been overclocking my brain, or maybe I was overambitious . . . but my faith in God was firm, and God did give me testimonies.

This book is a book of testimonies – and the stories of Lakshmi, Favour and Inger are but a few of the testimonies with which the Lord has coloured my ministry – but, even deeper than that, it is a book that explains why sharing your testimony is powerful. In the first chapter, biblical evidence is presented for grounding the need to tell your story. The rest of the book covers the topics that build on the foundations of the first chapter. You will discover that sharing your testimony acknowledges and proclaims Jesus in chapter two. In chapters three and four, you will find out how sharing your story can grow your faith and encourage others. In the final chapter, readers will explore the cosmic aspect of testimony sharing, as inspired by Revelation 12:11. You will find out how sharing your testimony helps in dispelling darkness and overcoming the devil.

This book is a way to redeem my pledge to God and to say, "Thank You, Jesus, for being there in my first year of pastoring." It is also a way to encourage fellow pilgrims with powerful stories and biblical evidence for the need to use your testimony to encourage others; to overcome the negative vicissitudes of life; and to look forward to when we all will sing the song of Moses and the Lamb. I invite you to take this short journey with me, prayerfully considering the biblical truths set out in the pages of this book. I also invite you to start believing in God for something big. Expect God to work in your life so that you can tell the memory of the great things He has done for you.

BECAUSE OF THEIR TESTIMONY

CHAPTER 1

"THEY WILL GIVE A TESTIMONY"

Psalm 145 is a fascinating psalm. It is not only the last psalm attributed to David but is also one of those six songs or hymns that close the book of Psalms itself. Moreover, it uses an acrostic pattern in Hebrew. According to a commentary by Willem VanGemeren, this psalm was recited twice every morning and once in the evening Jewish service. The Praise Psalm begins with an argument: God is wonderful and deserves to be the object of people's praise, day, and night, for ever and ever (145:1-3). Therefore, those who are aware of God's greatness ought to reflect on it and share it with others (4-7). In verse 7, according to the King James Version of the Bible (KJV), God's children "shall abundantly utter the memory of thy great goodness and shall sing of thy righteousness". In the Holman Christian Standard Bible (CSB), David explicitly says that God's children "will give a testimony of Your great goodness and will joyfully sing of Your righteousness".

Both the KJV and CSB versions of this Scripture text underscore David's prophetic words about God's children sharing the works of the Almighty with others. The text is a witness to what Christians do when they share a testimony in church or with others. For David, giving testimony of God's great goodness results in joyfully singing about His righteousness. This means that sharing our testimony of what God has done for us causes people to praise God and reflect on God's righteousness. Singing of God's righteousness, in both Hebrew and English, connotes singing fervently of God's justice or righteousness. It is as if children of God come together to declare that, even when we don't fully comprehend, God is always just and fair in everything He does.

I do not know about you, but for me Psalm 145:7 (recalling God's faithfulness and singing of His righteousness) foreshadows a kind of future activity. That future activity is captured in Revelation 15:3. It is the saints of God singing the song of Moses and the Lamb in Revelation 15:3. The NIV renders the text thus: they "sang the song of God's servant Moses and of the Lamb: 'Great and marvellous are your deeds, Lord God Almighty. Just and true are your ways, King of the nations.' " This song itself is a testimony of their redemption. John connects Moses' song in Exodus 15, which captures the redemption of the Israelites from bondage, with the sacrifice of Jesus as the Lamb who was sacrificed for our redemption from sin.

If this future activity is part of the action of the redeemed in heaven, I think Christians should take more time to reflect on our beautiful God and all that He has said and done while we are on earth. For me, every testimony here on earth is a kind of rehearsal of the grand demonstration of our gratefulness to the redemption song we as saints will sing in heaven before the heavenly beings. Therefore, we can participate in David's prophecy in both the here and now as well as in the hereafter.

Participating in David's prophecy in the here and now is not just a foretaste of the hereafter: it does remarkable things for the testimony giver and for the listener(s) in the present. First, sharing our testimony is a way to acknowledge God. This increases our faith in God, which then becomes a catalyst to grow other people's faith in God. Therefore, this act brings praises to God and makes both us and others wonder at His great righteous acts. This in turn reveals God's strength and dispels the strength of darkness.

A vivid demonstration of this is seen in Mark 5, in the exorcism of the demon-possessed man in the country of the Gadarenes. After Jesus healed him, he wanted to follow Jesus. However, Jesus did not allow him to come, but instructed him to "go home to your own people and tell them how much the Lord has done for you, and how he has had mercy on you" (verse 19, NIV). Mark concludes the story by reporting that when the man proclaimed to the Decapolis (that is, ten Greek cities on the eastern side of the Sea of Galilee, including Damascus), those who heard him "were amazed" (verse 20, NIV).

The Greek word used for "were amazed" is *thaumázo*, which means "to wonder, to marvel and to admire". It is the same word used when people marvelled at the miracles of Jesus. In fact, in Matthew 8:27, after Jesus calmed the storm, the Bible tells us that His disciples marvelled. This "marvelling" is close to praising God. It is more like the people were awestruck at what God had done. When people wonder about the acts of God, it is almost tantamount to singing His praise and righteousness. In essence, the people who heard of the exorcism the Lord had performed were awestricken, and most probably *wondered after Christ*. Therefore, Mark is telling us that the healing of the demon-possessed man is a story that exalts God and shows God's people how merciful and righteous God is. This undermined the power of darkness in those ten Greek cities in which the man proclaimed the Gospel of Christ.

Having set a biblical foundation for the need to testify of the things God has done in our lives, it is expedient to set forth four practical points as reasons for sharing our testimonies.

It Acknowledges and Proclaims Jesus

To acknowledge Jesus means to acknowledge His sacrifice on the cross, the one defining act of humanity's history. Our redemption in Christ would not have been possible without this sacrifice. This means that we would be nothing without Christ. Thus, acknowledging Christ recognises His power to save. It gives God all the glory due to Him, and by so doing we proclaim Christ as Lord to others, both Christians and non-Christians. As we will see in the next chapter, when we share our testimonies, we use the memory of what has happened to us to talk about who Jesus is. In addition, because we acknowledge Christ in our stories, the testimony we share becomes part of God's history (His story). God's history, or His story, is the salvation story. Therefore, acknowledging Christ not only proclaims Jesus, but it also gives us the opportunity to incorporate our stories into the Gospel of salvation for the world.

It Grows our Faith

It is colloquial to say that we grow our faith by listening and acting and praying on God's word. When we believe and practise our faith in God's word, we are in the process of growing our faith. At the same time, as we will read in chapter 3, when we follow the biblical command to tell of the goodness of God in our lives, we reinforce the word of God and ground it in our experience. Moreover, when we hear of the acts of God in the lives of others, we are pushed to trust God in those areas of our lives in which we have been waiting on God. By testifying about God's greatness, we praise God and reveal our appreciation. The result is a growing and deepening of our faith. Therefore, our capacity to believe is increased when we testify.

It Encourages Others

Sharing our testimonies has a double action. While it helps to increase our faith, it increases the faith of others and ultimately encourages them. As chapter 4 will reveal, our testimonies become resources for other believers to hold onto when believing in the possibility of a miracle in their lives. Those persons may be going through similar issues that you have overcome. Accordingly, you become a beacon of hope for them in both the present and the future. Therefore, people love to hear the great acts of God in the lives of fellow believers, because they get encouraged to keep pressing on.

It Overcomes the Enemy

Your testimony is a weapon the Lord has equipped you with to overcome the powers of darkness. When we praise God for what He has done for us in the past, we call upon His power for the present struggles and future victories. In the final chapter of this book, we will explore how Revelation 12:11 makes it clear that the saints overcame the devil not only by the blood of the Lamb, but also by the word of their testimony. Just as the testimony of the man formerly possessed by demons helped to bring light to the ten Greek cities, our stories – our memories of God's great wonders – bring light into the darkened corners of our lives, into our congregations, and into our daily activities.

What is your testimony? What marvellous deeds has God performed for you? Are you keeping them to yourself, or are you maybe only informing your closest friends and family? Jesus wants you to tell everyone about the beautiful things He has accomplished for you. Additionally, He wants you to share with them how compassionate He has been, to the point of dying for them. Declare that you are giving Him the praise He deserves. Come with me on this journey as we explore the reasons for sharing our testimonies.

CHAPTER 2

TESTIMONIES ACKNOWLEDGE AND PROCLAIM JESUS

Proverbs 3:6 (KJV) says, "In all thy ways acknowledge him, and he shall direct thy paths." The word "acknowledge" comes from the Hebrew word *yada*, which means "to know or recognise". In the case of Proverbs 3:6, we have been called to recognise that God is the ultimate Judge of our lives in everything we do. This implies that we recognise that Jesus is God, and we recognise His authority in what we are doing. In this vein we can understand Paul's words in proclaiming his testimony in 1 Corinthians 2:1-12, where he says that he has resolved to "know" or "recognise" nothing except Christ and Him crucified. This is what sharing our stories achieves. Let us use this biblical framework to understand what it means first to acknowledge Jesus and then to proclaim Him.

Testimonies Acknowledge Jesus

When we share our testimonies, we acknowledge the sacrifice of Jesus on the cross as that defining point in our own history and the shared history of humanity. This happens whether we testify of our salvation from sin, our conversion, a miracle in the health of a parent or child, or a breakthrough during an interview or application process. What we are doing is to eventually tell the listening world that there is a power higher than us without which we could not have achieved what we have achieved. That power is the power of Jesus. It was given to Him at the resurrection because He humbled Himself to the death on the cross, that at the mention of His name every knee must power. The knee of shame, the knee of pain, the knee of sadness in marriage, and the knee of spiritual drought bow at the mention and working of Jesus. Therefore, our testimonies acknowledge Christ and recognise His power to save.

As I said in the previous chapter, when we share our testimonies, we use the memory of what has happened to us to talk about who Jesus is. This is exactly what a fellow Adventist sister does, one whom I have come to respect as a devoted child of God. I have heard and read about her testimony in bits. One aspect of her story deals with how she became converted. Sister Lakshmi was born into a Hindu family. As Hindu devotees, her family members valued the various traditions and festivals of Diwali, Makar Sankranti, and Krishna Janmashtami, among others. When she was eight years old, her mother began attending meetings of a Christian community – the Seventh-day Adventist Church. The reason for this was that Lakshmi's mother had heard about a God who did not require anything to love and bless you. After some time, she began taking her children to church as well. Lakshmi was happy to join the children's Sabbath school, learning about Jesus, singing new songs, and reading about fascinating Bible stories. Even at a young age, Lakshmi discovered the difference between what she had believed before in Hinduism and what she was beginning to know in Christianity. She preferred to pitch her tent with the Jesus of the Bible, who was able to speak to her heart.

A turning point in the life of Lakshmi was when she began praying by herself. During this time, she learnt to memorise scripture texts. In particular, this exercise included memorising the psalms. She recalls that it was during this period of committing scripture to heart that the Holy Spirit convinced her of the truth. Thereafter, at the age of sixteen, she made a conscious decision to become a Christian and get baptised. Since then, Lakshmi has never regretted her decision to become a Christian. This is because the Word of God has taught her who Jesus is. According to her, knowing this helps us understand "why and for what purpose we are born into this world where nothing seems to make sense, and what will happen once we die. Knowing the truth, Jesus, has changed not only how I understand the world, but also who I am, and this faith in Him always holds me steadfast and gives me an eternal hope that no one else can give." Lakshmi does not fail to tell her story, telling how, though she may still observe some parts of the Indian culture, Christ remains the central part of her life and that of her family, as does sharing His love and what He has taught us.

Testimonies Proclaim Christ

Sharing our testimonies gives God all the glory due to Him, and by so doing we proclaim Christ as Lord to others, both Christians and non-Christians. This is the goal of Lakshmi. She is always eager to tell people of how God never abandoned her in her university days. One episode of her life that has served as a way to proclaim Christ to her friend is of interest. Lakshmi desired to study Geography and the Environment after high school. However, she missed the mark of getting a scholarship abroad. It seemed as if her dream had been dashed, because her home university did not offer Geography and the Environment as a study topic. Despite this, she never lost hope in God. She began working to save to study aboard. However, after one year of work, she could not raise enough money to go abroad. She settled for her home university. But God never fails those who trust in Him. In fact, God wanted to use her story to impact her best friend. Just at the time when she began applying for a course at her home university, the university board decided to begin offering Geography History. Her best friend called her to break the news. But she wanted to know how Lakshmi had been able to convince the university to offer the programme. "What have you done?" her best blurted out when she called Lakshmi; "I can't believe my eyes! This is the first time this year that this university is offering courses in History and Geography, exactly when you needed them!" It will interest you to know that the year Lakshmi applied to her home university was the only year that the university offered that programme option. Her story, which was unveiling itself before the eyes her non-Christian friend, became a way to witness of Christ.

Witnessing of Christ was what the man formerly possessed with demons achieved in Mark 5:19, 20 when he proclaimed his story in the Decapolis. He obeyed Christ by proclaiming Christ. The disciples also obeyed and proclaimed Christ. In Acts 1:8, Jesus said to them, "But you will receive power when the Holy Spirit comes on you; and you will be my witnesses in Jerusalem, and in all Judea and Samaria, and to the ends of the earth" (NIV). Indeed, when they received the Holy Spirit, they began proclaiming Christ. But notice that they did not just go about talking of doctrine or theology. They told the story of their encounter with Jesus. In fact, the book of Acts, in chapters 2-4, reports that they made sure to tell onlookers and authorities about Jesus, such that in Acts 4:13 the authorities recognised that the men had really been with Jesus. It is no wonder that, years later, the apostle John would argue the following:

> "That which was from the beginning, which we have heard, which we have seen with our eyes, which we have looked at and our hands have touched – this we proclaim concerning the Word of life. The life appeared; we have seen it and testify to it, and we proclaim to you the eternal life, which was with the Father and has appeared to us. We proclaim to you what we have seen and heard, so that you also may have fellowship with us. And our fellowship is with the Father and with his Son, Jesus Christ." (1 John 1:1-3, NIV.)

In this context, Ellen G. White encourages us to make sure that our witness is proclaiming Christ. She writes:

> As witnesses for Christ, we are to tell what we know, what we ourselves have seen and heard and felt. If we have been following Jesus step by step, we shall have something right to the point to tell concerning the way in which He has led us. We can tell how we have tested His promise, and found the promise true.

We can bear witness to what we have known of the grace of Christ. This is the witness for which our Lord calls, and for want of which the world is perishing. (*The Desire of Ages*, p. 340.)

Finally, because we acknowledge Christ in our stories, the testimony we share becomes part of God's history (His story). God's history, or His story, is the salvation story. Therefore, acknowledging Christ not only proclaims Jesus, but it also gives us the opportunity to engrave our stories in the salvation story of the world. Therefore, as the apostle John confirms in 1 John 1:1-3, we are encouraged to tell of what we have experienced in our lives – the power of God in redeeming us and in calling us into the ministry of telling others about Him. Yet, while we all have our individual stories of the great and marvellous works of God, we should be aware that this is not just another story. Our testimonies, witness and stories are grounded in God's own story. Knowing this and being aware of this, we should be aware that our stories carry a persuasive force because we are calling people to acknowledge God. In turn, listeners respond not to our story *per se*, but to what Christ has done as a result of our proclamation of Christ. This was the case with the former demon-possessed man in Mark 5, as it was with the apostles and Sister Lakshmi.

CHAPTER 3

TELLING OUR STORIES GROWS OUR FAITH

The King James Version of Romans 10:17 says, "So then faith cometh by hearing, and hearing by the word of God." This text presupposes that the planting of faith is a result of hearing and heeding God's word. Thus, the more we read, listen, and heed God's word, the more our faith grows. It is like going from one level of faith to another level of faith ("faith to faith"), as Paul argues earlier in his letter in Romans 1:17.

The Greek word for faith, *pistis*, means that someone has a commitment to someone. It can also mean a trust in or a dependence on someone or something. This means that, to increase our trust and commitment to and in God, Scripture is indispensable. Hence, a thorough understanding of faith acknowledges that the mind, heart, and will are all involved in ensuring our commitment to God.

This means that, to have a genuine faith in God, we need to read God's word. We also need to heed God's word. There is a third step, and that is testing or proving

God's word. If we read and heed God's word without testing His promises in Scripture, we may not mature fairly in faith. David prophesied that when God's children give a testimony of His great goodness, it will result in joyful singing of God's righteousness. He was indirectly telling us to test or prove and see. As a pastor, I am expected to dissect God's word, to teach it and to preach it. But I have come to understand that if I do not encourage God's children to test or prove God's word and His promises, my job is not complete. This is the reason why, when we follow the biblical command to tell of the goodness of God in our lives, we reinforce the word of God and ground it in our experience.

Inger's Testimony

I have heard about many Adventists who had issues with work on Sabbath or exams on Sabbath, and how they overcame by proving God's word. These stories were never vivid until I met Inger. I will tell more of Inger's story later in this book – yet an episode in her conversion caused my faith to increase. When she heard about the truth of the Sabbath – the need to keep the Sabbath day holy and not do any work – she determined to test God's word in Isaiah 58:13, 14:

" 'If you keep your feet from breaking the Sabbath and from doing as you please on my holy day, if you call the Sabbath a delight and the LORD's holy day honourable, and if you honour it by not going your own way and not doing as you please or speaking idle words, then *you will find your joy in the LORD*, and I will cause you to ride in triumph on the heights of the land and to feast on the inheritance of your father Jacob.' For the mouth of the LORD has spoken." (NIV.)

Inger told me that it was when she began heeding and proving God's promise that she found true joy in the Lord. She told me that at her workplace, which had employees doing shift work and expected everyone to work at least once a month on Saturdays, she insisted to work on Sundays instead. And when she found joy in keeping the Sabbath, she was not willing to give it up, even if her boss asked her again and again.

My Testimony

Hearing the testimony of Inger caused my faith to grow in many areas of my life and ministry. I could tell how I asked God to work on my bosses so that they could release me immediately to answer His calling as a pastor in Berlin. Normally, in Germany, you give three months' notice of resignation. I gave my notice in the middle of November, and by 1 January of the next year I was working as a pastor. I could also tell how God provided the car that our landlord brought to our doorstep, because God knew we needed a better one for the ministry in Berlin. There are many of those instances when I trusted God and proved His word, and He came through. But hearing the story of Inger caused my faith to grow concerning what God would do to enable my wife to give birth as the Hebrew women were said to. It is a wonderful miracle that has also caused my faith to grow as I shared it with my relatives, friends, and church members.

The New International Version of Exodus 1:19 tells us that the Hebrew midwives told Pharaoh, "Hebrew women are not like Egyptian women; they are vigorous and give birth before the midwives arrive." This text and the story around it have been told several times. In fact, people use it to pray for pregnant women. I also use it. But it became more vivid for me when, out of the blue, my wife had a complicated pregnancy.

Some months after we entered the ministry, she had become pregnant. The pregnancy was normal at the beginning. In fact, we would drive about 120 kilometres back and forth to Berlin at the beginning. I would also take her along for some of my visitations. It is true that the long drives may have caused a strain on her, but the complication developed the second night after we moved to Berlin. She had a dream in which a woman wanted to kick her stomach. We prayed about it, and then forgot about the dream in the morning. However, the next day she woke up bleeding. When the bleeding continued, I decided we should go to her gynaecologist. Early one morning, we drove to her gynaecologist, who worked almost 120 kilometres away. It was that day that we discovered she had placenta praevia.

Placenta praevia is a complication during pregnancy in which the placenta completely or partially covers the opening of the uterus, or the cervix. In my wife's case, the placenta completely covered the cervix. When a pregnant woman has placenta praevia, during labour and eventually at childbirth, there could be severe bleeding. This is because, when the baby enters the birth canal through the cervix, the blood veins that connect the placenta to the uterus may rip when the cervix starts to thin out (efface) and open (dilate). So the gynaecologist told us that there would have to be a C-section to deliver the baby. But we were told that there was a possibility that the placenta might go back to its normal position. However, to make us understand the nature of the problem, the doctor advised us not to have sex until after the baby's birth, which was to take place on 19 December.

I began reading about the whole thing and confirmed that possibility. So, when we changed gynaecologists and found one close to our home in Berlin, I asked about the position of the placenta. There was no good news. After several check-ups, we were told to go to the Charité Teaching Hospital to meet a specialist in childbirth. Aside from getting a specialist view on the matter, my wife's gynaecologist also wanted Charité to deal with the matter at childbirth in case any other complication came up. This was also in addition to the history of my wife's pregnancy. Our first son died in the womb at the end of the pregnancy. Our daughter had come into the world after my wife was offered an induction to catalyse the labour because the baby was too big.

After visiting Charité and listening to the professor, my wife became discouraged. She accepted the specialist view that she would undergo a C-section at childbirth. I remember telling her that the professor was not God, because God was the One who had called us to ministry. He was the One who had asked us to move to Berlin. He knew about the spiritual attack, and he could rewrite the future.

Prior to that moment, God had enabled me to minister by praying specially for pregnant women in my congregation. This came after I met a woman who was pregnant with twins, whom I prayed for, and after then I was sure to pray for other pregnant women too. When I told my congregation to keep praying for pregnant women, I never knew that my wife would need those prayers. Thus, I began praying for her. I prayed and rejected the professor's prognosis. I asked God to verify His word and enable my wife to give birth as the Hebrew midwives told Pharaoh that their women did.

Miraculously, the next appointment with the professor was cancelled. It was a miracle, because that was the date the professor wanted to give us an appointment for the C-section. But, for some reason, he was not available, and we had to pick another date. This also coincided with the local appointment with the gynaecologist towards the end of the pregnancy.

At the local appointment, I asked the gynaecologist to check the placenta, and she told us, to my joy, that the placenta had moved 1cm upwards. In the car, on the way back home, I told my unenthusiastic wife that I knew God would complete His work, because "he who began a good work in you will carry it on to completion" (Philippians 1:6, NIV).

After some days, we got an adjusted appointment at the Charité. This time we met with a different doctor or specialist. She was very patient in listening to us. I asked again about the placenta. For my wife, this matter was already settled, so she felt uncomfortable when I began asking about the placenta during the ultrasound. But I was acting on my faith in what God had promised. I was claiming a promise for my wife. Therefore, I had prayed during the previous nights and knocked on Heaven's doors. I pleaded with God to perform a miracle when we got to Charité. I think the challenge is that we do not ask enough, or do not knock; that is why sometimes we do not expect a miracle.

The doctor said she would check the placenta to see, since we had been told that there would be a C-section. When she checked, she told us the good news that the placenta had moved 2cm upwards. I asked what that meant. She said that, according to her specialist recommendation, there would be no need to perform a C-section, because 2cm was the limit. If there had been less than a 2cm movement, there would have to have been a C-section. We were scheduled for 7 December (not 19 December, the original date) so that my wife could come, be induced, and give birth.

My wife wanted by all means to give birth on 7 December, because it was my birthday. But God had another plan. On that day, when we got to the hospital after some early morning labour pains, they told us to go home, because there was no space. This was before a gynaecologist at the delivery section checked my wife. I was not allowed to be there, so I was outside, praying for God to complete what He had begun. The placenta had given way – now let the baby come! I was in prayer when my wife came out with her bags and said we were going home. Her sense of humour kicked in, and she began laughing. We laughed together, and I asked her what they had said inside the delivery department.

She was told by the gynaecologist who checked her to come the next day, because her cervix had not dilated enough (just about 2-3cm) for the delivery process to start. The idea was, when she came the next day, she would be induced to start the labour. God had other plans. He did not want our son to come on my birthday. Neither did He want any induction in this case. Hence, at 1.30am on 8 December, natural labour pains overtook my wife – and they were unbearable. We got to Charité shortly before 2.30am, and she was rushed to a delivery room. Our son was born at 4.30am, after my wife experienced labour like that reported of the Hebrew women and gave birth rather easily and quickly, to the surprise of the midwife who was attending her.

Now, the interesting part about the miracle is that, after our baby arrived, the placenta refused to come out. The doctor and the midwife came and did an ultrasound, and said the placenta had gone too high up in womb. I did not know if I should laugh or cry! What I did know was that the prayer I had prayed with my wife had been properly answered. After a couple of trials, the doctor told us she would have to perform a surgery to get the placenta out. I did not say anything, and neither did my wife, who was in severe pain after the childbirth.

What I did while carrying my son was to pray silently. I told God that if He had performed the miracle so that my wife could give birth naturally, why would He let this same placenta spoil the miracle He had begun? So, I asked Him to perfect it. Unbeknownst to me, my wife was full of faith, despite her pain, and was praying the same prayer. She told me that later. Soon, our delivery room was full of many nurses and midwives who tried several methods to get the placenta out. After many trials, the gynaecologist went out and brought the surgery papers for us to sign. But, when God begins something, He does not leave things half complete. It was at this time that a midwife came and tried acupuncture, and to our relief the placenta came out.

We called our son Chiedozie, meaning: "God has perfected". It is a derivative of my own name, Chigemezi Nnadozie, which means: "God will perfect things with this child". While my first name is given in the future tense, the second name is in the present. But with our son Chiedozie, I saw that God had already perfected everything with the boy He had given to us. He did not need to do it in the future but had already done it. Chiedozie's second name is Elian, meaning: "the Lord is God", which tells of the authority of God over all problems and issues.

I had told God that if He performed this miracle, I would write about it in the testimony book I was planning to write. I was not enthusiastic after the birth of Chiedozie anymore. But the more I told my mum, or a family friend, about what God had done, the more I saw them glorifying God. In turn, their praises influenced me. I wanted to keep my promise to God. And, just after writing this now, my faith is renewed, refreshed, and increased. Just retelling the account has given me a new cause for my faith in God to increase.

By testifying about God's greatness, we praise God and reveal our appreciation. The result is an ever-greater deepening of our faith. Therefore, our capacity to believe is increased when we testify. Our faith is bolstered as we venture outside of our comfort zone, because we must rely on God. This is a wonderful opportunity to put your trust in God, who alone has the power to win people to Himself.

CHAPTER 4
TELLING YOUR STORY ENCOURAGES OTHERS

Paul, in 1 Thessalonians 5:11, says: "Therefore encourage one another and build each other up . . ." (NIV). According to *Strong's Concordance*, the Greek term for "encourage" in the New Testament is *Oikodomē*, which also refers to any sort of building or the act of edifying another person in Christian learning, piety, happiness, or holiness.

One way to encourage, build or edify each other in the Christian journey is to share our experiences and our stories of triumph. In the Bible verse we are now looking at, the main reason Paul instructed the Thessalonians to encourage each other was so they might be ready for Christ's return, which may occur when least expected. Since the journey is not an easy one, words of encouragement can help a fellow pilgrim.

As we have read in the previous chapter, our testimonies help to increase our faith. But there is a further aspect to sharing our testimonies. It is the double action of our testimonies. Like a boomerang, while sharing our testimonies increases our faith, it also increases the faith of others, and ultimately encourages them.

The reason why our testimonies encourage others is because our testimonies become resources for other believers to hold onto when believing in the possibility of a miracle in their lives. Those persons may be going through similar issues that you have overcome. That was the case of a sister at my church who was pregnant with twins. The day I prayed for her was the day the Lord impressed on my heart to pray constantly for all the pregnant women in our church. But I did not know that my encounter and prayer for her would result in a glorious testimony that encouraged myself and my wife.

How Twin Foetuses Survived a Diagnosis of Down's Syndrome

One Wednesday afternoon, I was driving to church for a midweek prayer service. I got a call from Sister Favour, telling me she had had a successful delivery of her twin babies. I praised God with her and prayed. But she had not finished. She reminded me of the day I prayed for her and asked me if I had known she had a complication. I told her I had been unaware. She proceeded to tell me that, at some point in her pregnancy, she was strongly advised to have an abortion. The reasons were as follows.

One of the babies had a right-sided aortic arch. The aortic arch is a portion of the aorta in the heart that helps distribute blood to the head and upper extremities via the brachiocephalic, left carotid, and left subclavian arteries. The aortic arch is also involved in blood pressure homeostasis via baroreceptors in the walls of the aortic arch. A right-sided aortic arch is an uncommon heart problem among infant foetuses. The prenatal diagnosis was Down's syndrome for the foetus with the problem.

For the other baby, during an ultrasound, a white spot was discovered in the foetal heart. The medical term for this is "intracardiac echogenic focus" (ICEF). Some medical personnel claim that ICEF can disappear and may not be an issue for the baby. However, when the doctors discovered intracardiac echogenic focus, they also claimed the second baby had Down's syndrome. They wanted Favour to terminate the pregnancy. But this did not deter their mother from praying.

How do you deal with the news that your twin babies may both have Down's syndrome? Well, Favour knew that she had one solution. Favour would place her hands on her stomach and pray for her babies. She called on Jesus to do something about the matter. She trusted Jesus, and asked God that He might not fail her, since she was not heeding the call for abortion. And God did not fail her. After she delivered the twins, a paediatrician carried out a couple of examinations. The twins were pronounced healthy, although they had constricted vessels. The last time I spoke with Favour on the phone and after I visited her, she told me that her children were healthy. Hence, not only did she have a safe delivery without issues, but her children also did not have Down's syndrome and are developing well with the favour of God and man.

That Wednesday, after Favour shared her testimony with me, I remembered planning to tell the rest of the church in one of my sermons. But I also remembered asking the Lord to perform a miracle for my wife, as He had for this sister. Her testimony and story of triumph also became a source of hope and encouragement for us in our situation. While Inger's story helped me to trust God in His word and to claim His promise, Favour's story became a beacon of hope for us and served as a resource for us to hold onto while praying for our own issue. That is what happens when you share your testimony with others. You become a beacon of hope for them in both the present and the future. This is why people love to hear of the great acts of God in the lives of fellow believers – because they get encouraged to keep pressing on.

Leaving Everything to Follow Jesus?

Getting others to keep pressing on was what Inger achieved when she told bits of her story to her local church after her baptism. I still remember a lot of younger persons going up to her and thanking her for her testimony.

Before Inger got to know Christ personally and eventually got baptised, she lived her life in a reckless manner, even though she was a professed Christian. She built a career as a professional dancer. It was this that led her into various vices. She would go to parties, smoke, and drink alcohol when she was not working. At work she was introduced to several meditational practices that made her susceptible to darkness. When she taught her dance classes, she would introduce her students to yoga and deep meditation.

All of these came to end one day when she dropped to the floor unconscious while practicing for her dance classes. She reports that she experienced a supernatural activity, but this time from Jesus, who wanted her to stop everything and follow Him. From that moment on, she found her dusty Bible under the bed and began reading. Then the Lord led her to make some drastic decisions. She stopped drinking and smoking. She stopped dancing and teaching. She would not go to the club or parties. She had to end her relationship with her partner, with whom she was living. She basically started a new life.

While reading the Bible, she became convinced that the seventh day is the Sabbath of the Lord. This means

Saturday, and not Sunday. Subsequently, she began searching and asking God to lead her to the right church that keeps the Sabbath. When she found our New Life SDA Church, God provided a woman who helped her with the issue of accommodation. She found a job where she was allowed keep the Sabbath, and she began intensive Bible study towards baptism.

It was not an easy journey for Inger. She had to sofa-surf a few times with friends to finish her baptismal study, since she wanted to go home. Sometimes she would cry to the Lord and ask Him where He was taking her. She left everything for Him; she had had what seemed like a comfortable life before, and now things were difficult. She had left her career and did not know where to start in life.

During those difficult moments, we encouraged her to keep going. And she did. She got baptised in a beautiful ceremony and told her story to the rest of the church. After her baptism, when she moved to her home country, she told me how she had begun the process of talking to her family to tell them the reasons she had made a drastic change in her life.

They would resist, ask several questions, and she would try to explain from what she had learnt. She also found one or two persons outside her family to minister to through her story. When I look back, I think she was unconsciously following the command in 1 Peter 3:15: "Always be prepared to give an answer to everyone who asks you to give the reason for the hope that you have" (NIV).

Even before she went home, she began studying with her mother and a friend and telling them her story. Her story became a point of reference for many young adults in our church. It also became a source of hope to other believers, who became encouraged to keep pressing on towards the goal and prize set before us by our Lord Jesus.

CHAPTER 5
TESTIMONIES AND OVERCOMING THE ENEMY

In Revelation 12:11a, we are told that the saints of God overcame the beast in two ways: "They triumphed over him by the blood of the Lamb and by the word of their testimony" (NIV). The context of this text is Revelation 12. Revelation 12:7-12 is sandwiched between two parts of the story of the woman, which is the church of God, and the dragon, which is Satan. Revelation 12:7-12 describes a battle in heaven between Michael and His angels on one side, and the devil, formerly known as Lucifer, on the other. Before Lucifer was expelled from heaven, he had access to Heaven and engaged in accusing the believers there, as Job 1 demonstrates. After his expulsion, he began fighting a losing battle against Christ and His disciples.

Revelation 12:7-12 describes his fierce hostility to the virgin-born Son of God, as reported in verses 4 and 5; the Church; and Christ followers, as foretold in Genesis 3:15. Despite the devil's hostility, John reports that God's saints triumphed, or overcame the devil, by the blood of Jesus, the Lamb of Calvary, and by the word of their testimony. Often, we forget that this text has two elements by which the saints overcame the devil: the blood of the Lamb, and the word of their testimony. I do not need to convince any believing Christian about the potency of the blood of Jesus as the Lamb of God. It is the source of our redemption, against which Satan has no power, since the blood makes us righteous and saved.

But I would like to make a case for the second element: the word of their testimony. While believers can be saved from the devil by the blood of the Lamb, the testimony of believers also aids in overcoming the devil. If we firmly declare our faith in Jesus, the devil cannot prevail against us. That testimony in this context is the confession of faith in Jesus. It is maintaining that one's experiences have shown that there is no other person who holds our future except Jesus. It is glorifying God for what He has done in the past, what He is doing in the present, and what He will do in your life in the future.

The other dimension of overcoming by the word of their testimony is in reference to being faithful to Christ's witness during suffering and tribulations brought about by the devil. Believers who overcome are not swayed by death or persecution, such that when the devil scares them with such evil, they overcome him by adhering to the truth of their redemption, telling everyone that they do not love their lives more than the deed of Jesus Christ on Calvary (see Revelation 12:11b). That is why we hear stories of martyrs who did not back down when facing death, but remained steadfast in their devotion to their Saviour, leaving their final witness to the validity and influence of the Christian faith. That was how Christianity became established on the earth, and John in a vision saw the saints triumphantly doing so. He also saw the angels and the saved in heaven celebrating the victory.

Therefore, your testimony is a weapon the Lord has equipped you with to overcome the powers of darkness. When we glorify God for what He has done for us in the past, we are already calling upon His power for the present struggles and future victories. Let us now explore powerful stories that help illustrate this point.

Because of Their Testimony

We start with the story of Andrew, the brother of the apostle Peter. From early Christian history, we know that Andrew preached in the Black Sea region and had a hand in founding several churches. He was the missionary who started the church in Constantinople or Byzantium. Because of his faith, Andrew was crucified on an X-shaped cross on the southern coast of Greece. This crucifixion involved a cross similar to the one used to execute Jesus, but oriented differently, as Andrew refused to be crucified like Christ, because he felt unworthy of it. The story of Andrew's death is like that of his brother, Peter.

Peter was a powerful preacher who was prominently featured in the first half of the book of Acts, following the death of Christ. He established the church in Antioch and travelled, primarily to Jews, but also to Gentiles, to share the Gospel of Jesus Christ. During Nero's rule, Peter was arrested and ultimately faced martyrdom. He was crucified upside down. He is claimed, like his brother Andrew, to have objected to being crucified in the same fashion as Christ, because he felt unworthy of the same treatment.

Have you heard the story of Felix Manz? Felix Manz was a follower of Ulrich Zwingli, the Swiss reformer. However, Manz came to believe that there was no biblical mandate to practise infant baptism. In fact, he argued that those who do it follow the papists, whose practices the Reformation was intended to reform. On hearing about this, a council called Felix Manz and asked him to recant his view. He not only refused, but he also went and conducted adult baptisms, which was a crime in Zurich at that time. This infuriated the council, and the punishment for such "crimes" was drowning within two months.

Thus, Felix Manz was condemned to death. On the day of execution, while being led from prison to a boat, he gave praises to God and preached to onlookers. It is said that one of the priests tried convincing him to recant, but Felix Manz was encouraged by his brother and mother, who urged him to hold on to his beliefs. The authorities put him on a boat and tied his hands. They forced him to squat and immobilised him by placing a stick behind his knees and above his elbows. There, in the presence of his fellow Christians, he was drowned to death. His final words were: "Into Your hands, O Lord, I commit my spirit."

Finally, there is the story of Karl Georg Harress, a Seventh-day Adventist minister who died in a concentration camp during the time of the Third Reich in Germany. Pastor Harress caught the attention of Gestapo spies during his evangelistic meetings. In December 1941, Pastor Harress held a week of prayer. There he openly opposed the Nazi regime by quoting Daniel 2 to underscore the fact that no earthly kingdom will last. Unknown to Pastor Harress, there were undercover Gestapo agents in the crowd. After the programme, Pastor Harress was arrested.

During the intense police interrogation, he did not recant his views. In fact, he mentioned the curses of Deuteronomy 28, as well as Zechariah 2:8, where God cautions anyone who touches the apple of His eye, Israel. Therefore, having been taken into custody, he was brought before the people's court, where he was sentenced to a concentration camp. There he was made to clean footpaths with a toothbrush. Yes, a toothbrush! Consequently, he became very weak. But this did not deter the guards from beating him repeatedly because he refused to use the greeting "Heil Hitler". In this state, the body of Pastor Harress could not hold on any longer. Soon he died the death of a martyr.

The common denominator in the stories of all the believers above is the steadfastness of their faith in Jesus and what they believed. But one thing I need to mention is that while persecution fans the flame of Christian faith, martyrdom catalyses the faith of those who witness the death of the believers. So was it in the case of Andrew and Peter. The Christian faith spread fastest in the places they died.

As for Felix Manz, his belief in proper baptism by immersion also sustained the Christian group we know as Anabaptists today. Many Christians are encouraged by this to hold onto the biblical doctrine of baptism by immersion. The story of Karl Harress has been told several times among Adventists. It served to encourage believers during his time, and it is one of those stories that keep echoing among German Adventists.

All the stories above did and still do one thing. They show how past Christian believers overcame the enemy. They also show how light came into some areas formerly covered by darkness. Just as the testimony of the man formerly possessed by demons helped to bring light to the ten Greek cities, our stories – the memorials of God's great wonders – bring light into the darkened corners of our lives, our congregations, and our daily activities. We can overcome the enemy in our difficult times by the word of our testimony, just as Christian martyrs overcame because of their testimony.

EPILOGUE

After I had finished writing this manuscript, I was thinking of how to write the epilogue. God gave me two testimonies to share. The first is related to Inger. The other is related to a sister who fell unconscious after an infection she had acquired at childbirth in India.

I called Inger and shared with her that I had taken a few episodes of her story for this book. She was glad. She also told me that she was writing her conversion story. Then she told me something that I need to share with you.

After Inger was baptised, she moved away from Berlin, back to her home country. After she moved, things were not easy for her in the first few months. She wanted to practise her faith, but she also wanted to live in a city. She began praying for a job and began applying. In the meantime, she attended the local church in her town. Attending church was difficult due to irregular bus services on Saturday. As a result, she pleaded with her brother to drive her to church on Saturday.

After a while, she asked her brother to join her in attending church, since he drove her there. Her mum also began attending church. When she shared with me that her family was attending church with her, I did not believe it immediately, because I remembered she had experienced some initial hurdles with her family after becoming an Adventist. But now they were not only attending church, but they were also looking forward to going to church! On Fridays, they would ask her if church services would be held the next day, on Sabbath.

Inger also mentioned that she was part of a group that had begun some outreach plans in church to reach her small town. She said that she was still waiting for God to answer her prayer; but that, with her family going to church and the outreach plans they had set in place, she understood why God had not answered her prayer. Maybe He had answered her prayer with a different response than she had hoped for by not letting her move to the city.

While Inger was sharing all this with me, a thought struck me. God had brought her back home for a reason: first for her family, and then for her town. In fact, God had taken her back for her to be a kind of missionary to her own people. That day, I was so encouraged that I decided to share this episode in this book. I also planned to use it to motivate my congregation, to stimulate them towards thinking of ways to serve God just like Inger.

The other testimony I want to share to close this book is still unfolding, but it is a very powerful testimony that demonstrates the need for persistent prayer. We have just concluded our Ten Days of Prayer for the year; and, among the many testimonies, the testimony of a sister from India needs telling.

At the beginning of the Ten Days of Prayer, a female member of the multicultural congregation I pastor wrote a prayer request in one of our groups, asking for prayer for her sister. She mentioned that her sister, whom we will call "Sita", was in a critical condition due to an infection. I forwarded the prayer request to our Prayer Warriors group, and they began praying.

However, Sita fell unconscious after some time and was put on the ventilator. She needed to undergo one operation, and then another. The second operation could not be carried out, since her incision from the first had not completely healed due to the infection. Here is where this testimony gets interesting. Sita has four children, plus a two-week-old baby.

When I heard about Sita's predicament, I called her sister, who explained the situation to me. I assured her that the Lord would not fail her. I told her to read Psalm 91 and promised to keep praying. We prayed fervently for Sita during the Ten Days of Prayer. Every evening, we prayed on Zoom. The members of the prayer group of the congregation also prayed individually.

During this time, I was impressed to take time to intercede for Sita on my own. This came from the inspiration I received from Roger Morneau's experiences described in his book, *Incredible Answers to Prayer*. Then I prayed one midnight, and the next day I asked God to raise Sita from the pit of death, just as He had raised people through the prayers of Elijah, Elisha, and Peter. The next day, I called for a special prayer for Sita after we had ended the normal programme for the Ten Days of Prayer. That day, her sister wrote to let me know that Sita was beginning to respond to her medication. Then we prayed and interceded fervently for Sita.

Over the next day or so, Sita was removed from the ventilator. This was not just a miracle; it was an encouragement to the whole church, and especially to the Prayer Group. On Sabbath, when we had the finale of the Ten Days of Prayer, we prayed again for Sita, asking God to complete the work He had started, according to Philippians 1:6. On Sunday morning, her sister called me to tell that she was able to speak to Sita on the phone, and she said, "She is out of danger now." The testimony of Sita's miracle is still unfolding. Just before I sent this book to be printed, her sister wrote me to inform me that Sita has been reunited with her children and husband.

There are a few reasons why I have shared Sita's testimony in this book, even though it was not planned. I shared it because God knows how to surprise us. I also shared it because I believe it can be a way to encourage anyone reading it. I have also shared it because it is one powerful testimony of what God is doing in my ministry, and I do not want to keep silent about it. I shared it because if you read this, and the other stories of triumphs and miracles contained in this book, you can join God's children in overcoming the enemy . . . *Because of your/their Testimony*.

AFTERWORD

God is acting in the here and now in a generation where the Christian beliefs are challenged with questions concerning the authenticity of supernatural events in relation to logic, reason, and the need for scientific evidence. The temptation is to relegate such occurrences to the past. But in this book God takes centre stage in the interpreted actions; in fact, according to the book, these real testimonies describe how God acts and answers prayers. These are testimonies that beg to be seen, as they bring to light what God does and can do.

These testimonies do not consist of theology. Rather, they are oral testimonies addressed to Christian believers who experience the inner workings of the Holy Spirit. Sharing them motivates and encourages believers to grow in faith in areas of life and ministry, thus accomplishing our task as Christians.

The suggestion of the Samaritan woman concerning Jesus in John 4:29 – "come and see" – reverberates through the testimonies in this book. This aspect of telling or sharing lies deep in Pastor Chigemezi's heart. He is my best friend, whom I met at the Adventist seminary in Friedensau. In our darkest moments we have shared our experiences together, and what stands out from our encounters is Pastor Chigemezi's quest to pray and listen to the voice of God.

This is how he always is; he has been actively and passionately encouraging others to share their stories, including me. He successfully established prayer groups and Bible study groups in his home and enjoys a successful ministry as a pastor. It is with joy that I witness this passion in his book as he and his family invite us to share in these testimonies, which lay a foundation for others to *tell* and *share* their own stories.

–Robinson Onderi
Pastor, Seniorenheim Friedensau and Adventgemeinde Burg bei Magdeburg, Germany

Ingram Content Group UK Ltd.
Milton Keynes UK
UKHW010851100323
418370UK00004B/440